Praise for Driving

"Hicks's poems gather up the stories of family, those lost in war, a child killed by a boulder from an illegal strip mine, even the Opry's pickers and singers. Around them the mountains 'hold the sky where it belongs.' They hold these poems where they belong, as well, the bedrock of Hicks's language and vision."

— Kathryn Stripling Byer, former North Carolina poet laureate

"Jane Hicks's poems are a 'fierce serenade' paying homage to the world with compassionate observation and vivid, exact detail so achingly real we recognize our own in it, even as we are drawn to the particular people, places, and stories of Hicks's part of Appalachia: the Carter Family, an early twentieth-century woman missionary, the enchantments of 'deep hollows and steep fields,' the devastation of illegal strip mining, the abiding influence of a grandmother whose 'blood / . . . flows strong' in the poet. These poems are beautifully, painstakingly crafted from the 'heart-cache' of Hicks's life and words."

— Lisa Williams, author of *Woman Reading to the Sea*, winner of the Barnard Women Poets Prize

"This is a strong collection whose vitality derives from its crisp and particular language, its ample detail, and ultimately, its artful rendering of experiences that are authentically and memorably human. [These poems] are an appreciation of the sorrows and complexity of life not only in Appalachia, but anywhere."

— Richard Taylor, former Kentucky poet laureate

Driving with the Dead

Driving with the Dead

Poems

Jane Hicks (signature)

Jane Hicks

Foreword by George Ella Lyon

Lisa!
Please enjoy
these poems from
the mountain heart.
Jane

K UNIVERSITY PRESS OF KENTUCKY

Published by the University Press of Kentucky

Scholarly publisher for the Commonwealth,
serving Bellarmine University, Berea College, Centre
College of Kentucky, Eastern Kentucky University,
The Filson Historical Society, Georgetown College,
Kentucky Historical Society, Kentucky State University,
Morehead State University, Murray State University,
Northern Kentucky University, Transylvania University,
University of Kentucky, University of Louisville,
and Western Kentucky University.
All rights reserved.

Editorial and Sales Offices: The University Press of Kentucky
663 South Limestone Street, Lexington, Kentucky 40508-4008
www.kentuckypress.com

Library of Congress Cataloging-in-Publication Data

Hicks, Jane, 1952-
  [Poems. Selections]
  Driving with the dead : poems / Jane Hicks ; foreword by George Ella
Lyon.
      pages ; cm
  ISBN 978-0-8131-4555-6 (pbk. : acid-free paper) —
  ISBN 978-0-8131-4557-0 (pdf)— ISBN 978-0-8131-4556-3 (epub)
  I. Title.
  PS3608.I279A6 2014
  811'.6—dc23

                              2014007895

This book is printed on acid-free paper meeting
the requirements of the American National Standard
for Permanence in Paper for Printed Library Materials.

Manufactured in the United States of America.

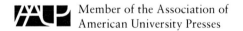
Member of the Association of
American University Presses

for Fern H. Huffman

The author's mother, Fern Hensley, age
eighteen.

Contents

Foreword

The title of Jane Hicks's second collection puts you on notice that you're about to read a book about loss. What it doesn't tell, however, is what distinguishes these poems: the lessons and wisdom the poet reckons from that loss.

Hicks clearly declares her purpose in "A Poet's Work": "the naming of what matters." Hers is not art for art's sake. She speaks out of the pain of the moment—meth labs, farm foreclosures, mountains devastated, mothers leaving for war. She also speaks against the greed at its root.

Fiercely set in Appalachia, these poems claim personal and cultural history, even as they speak out against forces that threaten both. "North Fork of the Holston 1962" evokes the river as Daniel Boone, the Cherokee, and A. P. Carter knew it, as well as the "green history" Hicks fished in as a child. But her gaze is not nostalgic. She goes on to name the businesses that have poisoned the Holston: Olin Saltworks, Eastman Chemical, Bemberg Rayon.

She takes Big Coal to task in two poems dedicated to Jeremy Davidson, the three-year-old crushed by a boulder that broke loose from an illegal strip mine operation and crashed through the roof while he slept. Similarly, she names those traveling with her who were lost to war: ancestors in the Great War and World War II, friends in Vietnam, folks called up by the National Guard today. Hicks cannot ignore "death's grotesque planting" and its harvest.

But the world in these poems is not without joy. In "What

Matters," Hicks catalogs pleasures from country ham to "flannel sheets," from "rusty dogwood" to "my chair near yours, a good poem." And always in her world, there is music. In "Poor Valley Pilgrims," she narrates the Carter Family's journey to make their first recording; "jolted," "rattled," "desperate," and "soggy," they come "to score/ the soundtrack of a nation." She glories in the "acoustic paradise" of "The Ryman Auditorium, 1965," where Mother Maybelle pulls her back to the heritage she was ready to throw off in favor of Elvis and the Beatles. In that moment, she is repatriated.

What she says outright in "A Transplant Leaves Minnesota, 1973," is a characteristic gesture of this collection:

I gleaned the remains of my life, turned toward the hills
that give me help, give me shelter,
hold the sky where it belongs.

With her grandmother's blood strong in her veins, her role as poet/seer affirmed by teacher and tradition, Jane Hicks speaks out for what matters most in "praise and remembrance."

George Ella Lyon

Driving with the Dead

Summer Rain

for Ron Rash

The second Sunday in July marks homecoming
at Pine Grove Freewill Baptist, celebrated not with football
and marching bands, but dinners on the ground
among our departed and a background of good gospel music,
down-home food, and talk of recipes, quilts, and bloodlines.

After a pooling of memory, my great aunts send me
to the old cemetery, where my great-great-grandfather rests
under an odd knob of quartz in a portion of graves marked with
    crude stones
beneath a row of ancient oaks that whisper and jostle in the breeze.

Out of the shade, in the heat of the new grounds marked
with flat bronzes, silk flowers, and American flags,
I see the stir and bob of balloons, and walk to where they lift and
    settle,
a chain of them, a card tied to the string to trace flight,
attract friends in far-flung places.

I stoop to retrieve the card, stub my toe upon my youth,
see the carved name of love that tasted of lake water and Juicy Fruit
on a blanket weighted with battered Keds and penny loafers.
A scratchy transistor soundtrack of *Dock of the Bay* and *Summer
    Rain,*
hourly newscasts of Chicago riots, assassinations of hope,
Hanoi, Haiphong, the burning of draft cards

like the new one in his pocket, all made me believe in nothing
but green eyes with little-boy lashes, summer-freckled skin,
smooth honeysuckle nights by the river with rain on the car roof.

He *suffered awful* in his mind, the aunties recall,
like so many that went over there. They detail
his end while we repack the bounty under rumbling threats.
I promise to replace the fieldstone with one that names my ancestor.

Rain lashes the windshield as I tune
in the oldies and *Forever Young* knifes my heart.
I retrieve the balloon card from my pocket and drive
toward the post office drop box to obey
the careful crayon message: *send me back.*

What Matters

Country ham, strong coffee,
hot biscuits, thick stew, mandarin sunsets
through bright windows.

Jack-in-the-pulpit, Trillium,
black Pawpaw blossom as we find spring,
green fiddleheads by the fencerow.

Night birds in soft summer,
familiar points on the sky map, red stars the heart
of the Scorpion and Eye of the Bull, a shared blanket.

Flannel sheets, my hand-stitched quilts,
star-speckled skylights, snow swirl,
down pillows.

Rusty dogwoods, flames of maple,
cider clean and bright on the tongue,
red sweet jam, summer in a jar.

Slow fire, wood smoke, high lonesome
bluegrass, a dog-eared favorite,
my chair near yours, a good poem.

Walking Boundaries

I part the fog, a wet veil against the sun.
Stained pink with morning,
curtains lift on dew-sparkle.

Night weavers hang prisms on crepe
myrtle and early-turned dogwoods.

The pasture grows waist-high where
Queen of the Meadow holds stately sway
over the cusp of autumn, witness to nutfall,
leaf drop, drone of dirt daubers
wrapping spiders in mud brick lairs,
spring calves grown summer fat.

The fencerows stand strong after
August night storms stripped sycamores,
lashed my windows with willows.

The sun mounts the ridge, boils away mist,
blazes bright on summer grown wildest
before it dims, cools, curls up for the long night.

A Transplant Leaves Minnesota, 1973

Miles and miles and miles behind me,
grain elevators mocked my retreat,
stark sentries in my rearview mirror.

I lost them at dusk when I drove in to the first
ripples of Wisconsin. The bowl of heaven arched
infinite over the featureless plains—blazed a searing blue
or transformed to a gyrating beast throwing bolts,
turning loose its spawn, tearing down
what was built up on the vast pastures.

I remember they dragged me to the cellar, I clutched my son
as the herd stampeded above, how we came to the light
and found rubble, pink house planks strewn for miles.
I gleaned the remains of my life, turned toward the hills
that give me help, give me shelter,
hold the sky where it belongs.

The Ryman Auditorium, 1965

I pouted and whined the whole three hundred miles,
would have kicked and screamed, except a sound
spanking follow. While Ed Sullivan touted the Beatles,
Elvis swiveled across the silver screen, Daddy savored
the High Lonesome on thick 78s and slow turning
albums. Bill Monroe, Jimmy Martin, droning banjos,
chirpy mandolins, crying fiddles drowned out
my Rolling Stones. Our family flew down Bloody 11-W,
rain-slicked and glittery, toward Nashville to sit
on curved church benches high in the Confederate Gallery
where funeral home fans pumped frantic rhythms to G-runs,
arthritic elbows bumped smooth-skinned young,
Beatle bangs mixed with brush cuts, lost in acoustic paradise.
I fumed, muttered, and strained to sit still. Flatt and Scruggs
ripped a swift set, caught my ear, then called her out to play
what my heart and bones remembered. Elvis and Paul forgotten,
I gave into melody and line, riveted to that pew
while Maybelle whipped that guitar into submission.

Roy

My grandfather wore a Stetson, not the cowboy kind,
but a felt fedora, ribbon banded, the inside leather embossed
with his golden initials. One resided in an old-fashioned
box taken out for dress, one he wore daily at dapper tilt
even with farmer overalls. The latter sat atop his casket
among the roses with the flag and doughboy helmet
that traveled to France and back. The fedora inhabits
my writing room, bears the scent of Bay Rum,
cigar and wood smoke, memento of a man
who read of the Wright Brothers in the paper, whipped
the Kaiser, sent his sons to hunt Hitler, patted
the porch swing and made room for his blue-eyed darling
as we hummed to the Opry radio, tin-roof rain drumming
while hounds on the ridges crooned the high lonesome.

The author's grandfather, Roy Hensley, c. 1938,
Greene County, Tennessee.

Poor Valley Pilgrims

July 31, 1927

July bore down like the devil's thumb,
thunderheads crouched on Clinch Mountain,
Queen of the Meadow and Ironweed
dozed in dusty ditches and fencerows,
heat shimmers swam with swallowtails,
and tiny white butterflies fanned at near-dry puddles
on the rutted wagon road where Black-eyed Susans
gave sly winks to A. P. Carter's folly.

He packed a borrowed car with his wife, Baby Joe,
Little Gladys, cousin Maybelle, and a borrowed
guitar to seek fame in song. They fled
Poor Valley for Jett Gap to ford the Holston River
before rain trapped them in grease-slick mud,
then twenty-six miles of gravel road hell,
the car tires, in summer molt, shed twice on the way.

The desperate pilgrims arrived
jolted and rattled at sister Vergie's door,
a soggy squalling baby, his milk-wet mother,
cranky sister, a pregnant guitar player,
and a dreamer ready to score
the soundtrack for a nation.

Revelation

Someone touched me as I dreamed
of ruined splendor

scent of crushed fern underfoot.
A tentative touch, a stroked arm, an embrace,

I extended my hand, awoke
heart-hammered and breathless.

Someone who matters must leave
my world, the embrace a certain farewell,

the intention no mistake of sleep,
no deceit of dream. Sure, defined.

Draft Lottery

July 1, 1970

Behind the meat locker, crammed into a tiny office,
the staff of the Taco King huddled about
a blurry black and white screen. Larry's
4F, polio-twisted hand held mine, I held Terry's,
Charlene held fast to Dennis, sweat dripped
from his nose, the drops mirrored blue shadows
on his forehead and around his eyes.
Paul, younger and trying for West Point,
stood guard for customers.

Fate circled and spun, old men called up
the young. The lives of Dennis, Charlene's young husband,
my boyfriend, and Terry tumbled in two cages,
numbers drawn at random. July gripped the pavement,
hunkered down and hovered, the Hardees across
the parking lot shimmered a mirage, the world
beyond a blur. No customers came, perhaps glued
to televisions numbering their sons.

July 9, the first call, my birthday. If a boy, I would have packed
for induction or Canada. We stifled nervous giggles as the
draw droned on: Number 22, Dennis out of school, out of options,
slid to the floor. We pulled him out of the close air,
Paul took him. Number 57 called Charlene's husband,
she gripped her belly, shaking. We quit watching at 150,
Terry's number, my boyfriend's never called.

In the light, Paul cradled Dennis,
spread cold paper towels across his peachy freckles.

We grew up trained to duck and cover, wary of
Sputnik's eye. The red glare of Mars raged greedy that year.
Paul climbed to West Point, Dennis came home with a habit,
Charlene's baby never saw his father, a bumper crop from the crew
that huddled behind the meat locker at the Taco King.

North Fork of the Holston, 1962

On Sunny View Drive, we lived
at the end of the road, wide fields,
deep woods stood where gravel stopped.

Up Mr. Smith's poplar-topped hill,
through barbed wire, out the saddle
of a ridged hay field, ran the path to

the Holston River. Green history flowed smooth
between limestone bluffs and sycamore banks,
past the baptizing grounds below Cloud's Ford

or back upstream to Poor Valley
where A.P. Carter collected songs we still sing,
downstream, the Long Island treaty grounds of the Cherokee.

We fled the sunny view for the cool one,
our candy striped floats bobbed on cane poles
as we jogged down the path to the Holston,

my brother in front, me in the rear,
heroes caped with towels, we sought the cool
water now mercury-poisoned

by Olin Saltworks on the north, merged
with Eastman Chemical spill to meet
the foul of Bemberg Rayon on the south fork
where Overmountain Men mustered at Watauga.

The gravel roads, now paved and marked,
run across subdivided fields of pretension
with a view of the deadly green flow.

Black Mountain Breakdown

Jeremy Davidson, 2001–2004

There are no outward signs of mayhem here
at the foot of Black Mountain. Things rest
as we left them, a plastic baseball glows
in the grass where you dropped it when mama called
for supper, a tricycle hides under the high deck
of the porch, a wading pool droops, leaf littered,
frozen. Inside, see the couch where you tumbled
with your brother, your video games abandoned,
your room marked with yellow tape, your crib
where you breathed easy as mama put you down to rest,
driven into the floor by strip-mine spoil,
your brother's room littered with bright Christmas
dragged from the closet as the boulder dozed through,
squatted by his bed, spared him but memory and nightmare.

The Color of Loss

for Barry and Larry

It's the dark inside a grape, a bruise,
storm clouds purpling an afternoon
grown cross with heat. It's a shadow
under the porch, blackberries stored in
dark cellars, a pond bottom,
shapes moving in the deep.
It's a moonless hollow, the underside of
owl's wing, clotted fur after screeched skirmish,
two huddled shadows in a porch swing,
one egg, two breaths, one soul.
It's a stain on fine linen after funeral food,
dark-papered dining rooms, high ceilings,
candles burned to sooty stubs.
It's an empty pillow, a tangled
deathbed, the shadowed eyes of the twin
who stares long into the night and waits
his still half to speak.

Expatriate

for Ron Hicks and Pvt. Oliver H. Hicks

There was no grave where the boy knelt
to drop salty sorrow or touch cold stone.
His father expatriated to Normandy
to reside in a colony of Yanks,
star-decked, under white crosses,
petroglyphs of nomination and rank.

Grief stalked the night,
bedcovers became foxholes,
thunder and lightning,
German artillery.
The child crouched,
pillows piled high
to imagine deep
French mud while
death zipped aloft,
plowed the soil above,
ready for grotesque planting.

The telegram hangs over her bed,
a photo with her boy's same face,
cap set at a jaunty non-regulation angle,
and the photo of his seaside
home, manicured and maintained
by French hosts in gratitude for duty.

France Oct. 2 6, 1918

The author's grandfather, Pvt. Roy Hensley, in France, October 26, 1918; he sent this postcard to his mother for Christmas.

Lietuva

(Lithuania)

for Danuté and her Papa

Dust motes settle, the day works
the cuckoo harder. Papa, your memory
hovers above my keyboard,
all smile and sad eyes. I remember sawdust
on your forehead like a priest's
thumb on Ash Wednesday, how you caressed
an emerging table leg with a tack cloth,
attentive to each lathed detail,
a hummed folk tune from a place
you cannot remember, stories given
you by the old ones: how the Nazis
came at last for the Catholics,
your entire family loaded
onto a manure-shrouded truck,
a last-minute dash from the forest
gave your mother heart to toss
you to an uncle's sturdy arms
as she collapsed under the weight
of good-bye, your first memories
formed far from her sacrifice.
You sang in her honor, made poems
for those who survived Hitler and Stalin,
sang praise to potatoes, dark bread,
and the Host upon the tongue,
in neat notebooks that I tap
into the keyboard, a rosary of memory.

Kindergarten

Beanie bears, balloons, pinwheels,
little lambs litter plush grass.
Bedraggled ribbons, papers, toys
faded by the elements, the clutter
of untended children among small tablets
evenly spread as nursery cots,
close-spaced as the desks of that strict
teacher none avoid. A gentle Jesus
glows in marble elegance, arms wide
to suffer this garden of children
inside the cemetery gate.

Color

Through indigo eyes she viewed a world of color, moved through
its palette: bright aprons over a housedress in shades of red or
    purple,
always a poke bonnet to match.

Her razored hoe scratched a rhythm among green beans,
fat striped squash, tomatoes of red and yellow. Scarlet hibiscus
flamed near the back steps where she threw out dishwater.
Petunias, lantanas, begonias, and her prize dahlias
basked in a garden of their own, became the templates for quilts
that grew from a scrap basket onto her lap.

She had a red couch, not sedate wine or burgundy, bold
"Good Golly" red with patchwork pillows. Remnants and bolts
stacked on a spare bed flashed a rainbow of 60s neon pink and
    green
sewed by pattern from Simplicity and McCall's for country girls
    craving
American Bandstand fashions.

I see her still, a mouthful of pins, her apron pierced
by threaded needles, her hands on bright
fabric or up to her elbows in cherries or peaches to fill aqua jars.

Near dark, blue shadows crept up the mountain as she worked
her butter, golden yellow pats marked with holly leaves from
weathered oaken molds, foamy milk, warm from the beast,

cools in the cellar, cream separated from the milk yields
buttermilk marked with flecks of gold.

We found her felled among pink peonies, clutching scissors.
"Bury me in purple," she said.
The church tongues wagged but we did.
She rests in mulberry silk with violets in her hands.

The home of Roy and Chlodia Hensley, Greene County, Tennessee, 1958.

Leavings

An engine block sagged the porch
last we visited. Piles of rubble and rock
now mark the smokehouse, rough boards carry
smells of salt pork and hickory. Root cellar damp
feeds morning glories, faces to the sun, once the scourge
of bean vine and corn stalk, where a sharp hoe flashed
in the garden rows, the odd volunteer vegetable
flourishes amid the ragweed.

Now engine block, broken porch, tin-topped house
disappear under the bulk of a mammoth metal
barn sprawled in the sun. Yellow jackets drone
at the ruin of pears while two goats clear the still-fenced
garden space, chew down wildness, turn golden eyes
on visitors who dare enter.

At garden's edge, just out of goat-reach, blaze
defiant dahlias, essentials of cemetery decorations and
church altars, bought, swapped and traded by those
gardeners who must be startled to now lie under
silk flowers on Styrofoam blocks. Dahlias grown
big as dinner plates, sisters in lavender,
peach and lemon, survivors, all blooded at the throat.

Drive by Slowly

Four rooms and a bath clung cliff-style
to Possum Ridge. The back porch closed in
for a boy's room later housed the piano,
the basement footed and finished for teens
grown tall enough to look fear in the eye,
take it on, push back. The side yard where
cinder block walls loomed, a garage stillborn
when the money hung about the neck of first
one woman, then the other
who shifted our foundation.

Roses still trail the eaves, the house joined
to finished rooms and a garage, double its
size under long-leaf pines, strangers brought on
from another place, freakish needles whisper,
whisper, taking root where the planter did not.

Glitter

We were to be dropped at Bible school, Mama insisted,
standing firm in her tomato-splattered apron,
since he was going out and her last batch of beans
wasn't done. Spit-shined and polished, our feet
on towels, we took our first ride in that cream-colored
Buick, a push-button automatic with leather seats
that smelled of smoke and Old Spice, arrow-sleek,
nothing like the cow-like Chevy station wagon, cloth seats
heavy with the remnants of ball practice, swim lessons,
and trips to my grandparents' farm and blue mud creek.
We watched his jaw work to pop and crack gum like
fireworks as we slid into the Minute Market
parking lot for what I figured to be a carton
of Luckies, next to a shimmering green convertible
cool as lake water and a redhead all done up in white.
Her earrings glittered as she strutted to the rear of the cars
where a terse and profane conversation preceded our peel out,
swift deposition on the church steps, and wink
of tail lights as he followed the green car toward town.

Jones and Thomason, General Merchandise

After they tore down my great-uncle's store,
the footprint of the foundation seemed so small,
the house smaller, his orchard, a scrap.
The store and grounds once seemed a universe,
a cool cave of memories, red asbestos shingles,
acres of tin roof, wide covered porch
that held dozens of loafers on a rainy day,
Saturday morning gleaners of news and nonsense.
Midwinter, they guarded the giant stove
that swallowed mounds of bituminous binned
out back, summer home of copperheads,
red wasps, and giant spiders. A barber chair
gathered dust by the drink cooler,
Nehis and Royal Crowns shoulder-deep
in frigid water, chest lid revealed jewel
bright bottle caps. A candy case
filled with Baby Ruths, Snickers, Mars bars,
loose candies to fill "penny pokes," our
parting treat. Near Christmas, bushel boxes
held creme drops, hard ribbons, orange slices
sugared and tart, pink and yellow bon bons for
scooping into stockings, always bon bons
for me, creme drops for my brother.
To one side, barrels of nails for horseshoes,
houses, and barn building, fence staples,
shingles, feed, seed, and in spring, baby chicks,
a yellow confusion of whirs and peeps,

a show in the spotlight of the heat lamp.
Broad stairs to a mezzanine of dry goods,
fabric on bright bolts, spooled thread,
rick rack, pins, and zippers. Overalls, boots,
hats, even once, a pair of black patent
Mary Janes—magically my size—the Easter Daddy
lay in the hospital. Around and back down,
a cold case of oleo and bartered butter,
brown eggs and yards of bologna
to be thick-sliced, carried home or heaped
into hearty sandwiches, round cheeses,
and slab bacon. Out back, the gray
shingled house that held dozens of mechanical
toys, some ancient, all working, that needed
to be touched, wound, and used in this house
of no children. A cool orchard with a white
bridge for foot dangling, toe swishing,
popsicle reverie, safe from all but
errant bees seeking hives that hummed
a fierce serenade.

Jones & Thomason General Merchandise, Pine Grove,
Tennessee, 1958. Wilbur Thomason reading gas pumps.

My Second-Grade Teacher Reads Gerard Manley Hopkins

At art time, we crafted Christmas paper, careful-kept,
reborn as tissue kites. Tethered rainbows with tattered tails
climbed into March, darted and leapt over playground minions.

A hawk on thermals glided, soared, swooped among the kites,
winged away, climbed high to wheel and hover, all below
    transfixed.
Back inside, teacher plucked a book from her shelf of verse,
"Listen with your heart," she said. "Ride the words
like a hawk rides the wind or kites dance free."

So I rode words that galloped on springs, swept off, soared again,
fell into now, cloaked in *vermilion,*
newest in my heart-cache of words.

Close Order

Fern's feet do not reach the floor
yet she sits in the upper level
at Pyburn School, in the shadow
of Chimney Top Mountain. Her dark
eyes measure the tree shadow, compute
the height, the formula new and anxious
to be tried. She figures corn bushels in the crib,
tallies the bill at Uncle Wilbur's store
before he can ring it in the great register.
Numbers march for her, swift and sure,
measure the world.

Exam papers tallied, she exits eighth grade,
dreams of high school ten miles down
the creekbed to the all-weather road.
She is eleven and does not know
she will not attend the school
that refuses a scrawny, underage girl
who chops corn, tops tobacco, captures
gardens in endless rows of pale green jars
until the town textile mill calls
her at eighteen to pack her bags,
walk out of the holler to become the
right hand of the plant foreman
who does not hear the song of numbers
in bobbin whine and loom clack.

She trains his tallies, rights his orders,
moves from hairnets and brogans

to neat ledgers and spectator pumps
in the front office where numbers
march and drill to her order.

"Wedding gift for Nola." Tennessee Eastman Company, Kingsport, Tennessee, c. 1948. Author's mother is in the fourth row up, second from the right.

A postcard sent to the author's brother from his second-grade teacher, Myrtle Foust, in 1962. The author is mentioned in the text of the postcard.

The Missionary

Myrtle Foust, 1902–1990

In her rented room, she makes tea on a hot plate,
a scribe bent over the word, to illuminate
slim, yellow grade books with precise
blue and red, as she measures and weighs
progress in her crusade against ignorance.

Her artist's hands soft, a ringless
map of veins, copy page upon page of poetry
in neat script on dime-store tablets.
She slips the tiny pages into a well-chosen
card on each student's birthday until
they reach eighteen, each card, each poem
as individual as the hands that open them.

One boy received his last missive
wrinkled, creased, much forwarded,
in-country, fifteen clicks from nowhere.
Soaked and stoned, he wept,
Kipling's "If" became a litany for sanity,
his benediction for safe return.

How many poems she sent as apostles
of the word—"The Windhover," "A narrow fellow
in the grass," March with his purple shoes—all taught
the fierce frolic of language and
the heartbeat of words.

From the bus stop, she strides up Flanders Street,
laced-up oxfords, a flowered shirtwaist,
her plastic rain cap clear origami armor
for permed curls. She takes up her pulpit,
reads the morning poem for all who would hear.

The Grace of Risen Dough

In death, my mother will stand elbow deep
in the yeasty flesh of dough as she did
five school days a week for over twenty years.
A stainless baker's table with three gleaming walls
holds the bounty she embraces, folds,
kneads, and pinches into trays and trays of air-
light rolls that even the pickiest eaters anticipate.
"It's pretty work," she says, "to watch the dough
rise, to work it, shape it, and watch the tops grow
delicious brown. Kind of like raising kids," she laughs.
She will set sacks of leftovers outside
the back door, nothing said, for those
who have no other supper, no heart to throw away
what might be needed. She believes
in a waiting time before Heaven,
work to be done before rest, so she will do
what she knows, embrace her work,
feed us all.

The wonderful lunch ladies at Temple Star School, Sullivan County, Tennessee. The author's mother, the manager, is on the far right.

Domestic Arts

When Pap started to roam, family legend goes,
Mam—my mama's mama—sawed nearly through the metal braces
under his galluses, his shoe strings the same;
only a scant stitch basted on his sleeves and buttons.
After a nip of shine, Pap cut loose a buck and wing,
flew apart on the dance floor, near naked,
buttons bounded to every corner, became
a local legend. He never mentioned it,
nor did she.

Mam trained Mama in the domestic arts.
She hacked apart Daddy's leisure suit, basted
that polyester nightmare top and bottom,
unscrewed the acrylic platform shoe heels
that once held live goldfish and replaced them
with cockroaches. First time he hustled some honey,
he molted, buttons flew, disco ball glinting
off his sweaty chest and chains, his split pants
open to the world. He never mentioned it,
nor did she.

Stay close, beloved. I inherited
Mam's sewing box, handed down
by a family of women
big on tradition.

My Grandmother Escapes

She made it four miles down Highway 21,
almost to Sebastopol, barefoot on Mississippi blacktop
in her petticoat, dangling a Styrofoam pitcher like a purse.
I pulled alongside and coaxed her into the car
by telling her "some man might get her."

She offered me peppermint from her pitcher and we drove
in silence. Her tangled and plaqued neurons
choked the speech from her. I was relieved, for nothing
good ever came from it. I stood too tall, too bookish,
too hillbilly compared to my cousins who spoke her drawl.

She drifts off and appears to ungrow. Always tiny,
made smaller in sleep, her mouth made soft, finally,
in having no words. An orderly brings a chair,
she does not wake when he straps her in. She curls to one side
as he wheels her back to dreams.

New Testament

Home from the hospital, swaddled in her quilts,
my grandmother decided I should know her worst,
that her grandmother never married.

I never said I read the census, worked out
the tree, found the broken limb, alien fruit.

There would be a horse, she whispered,
tied to the gate late night, soon another
red-haired boy, bold and big.

She did what she wanted, always proud
in her body, in her mind, free with herself,
never bowed before the Lord.
Unto the tenth generation, we are bastards.

The old Bible, I reminded, Moses and David,
the words of the New gentle for lovers
of the Lord. She meditated on this, wiped
her cheek, let go the need for fear.

Dismissal

The spring I left my husband,
Mother dismissed my father,
parked his boat in the drive,
loaded it with packrat plunder:
boxes of pamphlets, buttons, books,
bumper stickers all lauding
George Wallace and John Birch,
fishing rods, reels, shotguns,
hunting coats, Red Wing boots,
the stiff starched shirts and sharp
creased pants he demanded,
the black book he believed secret,
dismembered and scattered over the mess,
his Ku Klux Klan hood perched
like a jaunty cap on the motor.
Locks changed, doors barred, she ignored
his outraged pounding, drowned out
by Marty Robbins on the stereo,
watched the boat trailer bounce
on the gravel road, strewing
dusty propaganda in its wake.

Mordant

For weeks, we combed hillside, creek bank,
and fencerow for blossom, root, and husk
gathered in burlap and baskets boiled, stirred,
simmered with lye, salt, soda ash:
mordants that fix beauty and require fibers remember
madder red, golden yellow, walnut brown,
and Nature's loveliest prank,
pink from lacy, gray-green lichen.

The wind bites past the clothesline
looped with tangles of yarn and billows
of fabric drawn from white enamel pans,
black iron kettles, and galvanized tubs perched astraddle
three hearth stones each—the Mayan symbol of womanhood.

My mountain grandmother knows nothing of the Maya
but kens the pragmatics of balance in a three-stone hearth
on this day of low skies, brown leaves, and bare limbs,
a winter's work of bright sweaters, socks, and bedclothes
waving in the November wind.

The author (lower left), her brother (upper left), and their cousins celebrate Christmas, 1957.

Cousins

Until she died, my grandmother scanned the highway
for their car, as if she knew what they might drive.
We still don't know why they holed up in the house
where I was born, went to work, came home,
denied us all, denied the world, buried their mother
with no services, no visitation for respect.

The eldest, at least a churchgoer, announced in Sunday School
she was to have surgery. A week later, she was deposited
next to her mother in the same perfunctory manner. I sent roses,
remembered soft curls and brown eyes of my playmate who
dreamed of teaching. I left a card and received a cordial note from
her sister, who did not answer the door when I knocked.

Tonic

The wind cuts, my nose drips,
my fingers burn then numb,
gloves left behind in the almost April.

On my grandmother's old land,
the new owner knows my purpose,
waves me on to the fields
spotted with new growth.

With trowel and paper sack,
I seek that dark green delicacy,
creecy greens, dry land cress,
served with vinegar and egg
to purify slow winter blood.

My grandmother's habit urges me
out toward spring
that lies in fat buds at field's
edge, redbuds and dogwoods wait
for the call of sunlight.

Though ice laces creek banks,
young frogs peep as shadows grow long,
the clouds slow down. I think
of a warm kitchen, cornbread,
and bitter greens
cleansing my grandmother's blood,
which flows strong in me.

The Big Beautiful

for Pam Duncan

I fled the cloy of candles and lilies
to a dead-end road, to the tang of scrub pine
and salt air. Where earth, sky, and water
meet and breathe a primal tug and flow,
my brain cooled, muscles loosened,
blood sang back to the wind. I freed
my hair, pin by pin from the veil
that bound it, lace floated free
to shroud driftwood, my sister,
cast here by fortune and forces.
Night settled serene and perfect,
folded me into the big beautiful.

A country burial, Greene County, Tennessee, early 1950s.

Commencement Day, 2005

Diamonds and Rust undid me there on I-81,
dirge of old loves and slights keened
across from speaker to speaker, plaintive
Baez vibrato hung in the air, like your yearbook
face in my file of memories. So hopeful,
so eager to commence, your cap and gown tossed
to the backseat for tomorrow while careless boys
dove from the dock, brave of chilly May lakes,
and watched you cramp then sink into bottom-tangle of trees.
Three days down, at your parents' request, we gathered
the seniors, sent them forward, while your family stood
vigil lakeside. You remain forever new, no diamonds,
no rust, no memories gathered to cut you through
or break your heart.

A Poet's Work

for Jeremy Davidson, 2001–2004

> The aim of the poet and the poetry is finally to be of service,
> to ply the effort of the individual work in to the larger work
> of the community as a whole.
>
> —Seamus Heaney

Spare me the postmodern pout
about dog piss in the gray snow
near the subway entrance

or the academic angst over a shaft
of light like the one in a scriptorium
of an obscure Tuscan monastery.

Witness meth labs that spring up in our rural
gardens, a quick payout or fuel for three
piddly jobs, two to live, one to pay daycare.

Clutch the child who sobs silently,
her mama a nurse in the Guard, called up,
goodnights a webcam image from Basra.

Behold mountaintops removed, laid low by greed,
hollows filled, wells poisoned, God's majesty
flattened, fit only for Wal-Mart, the new Ground Zero.

Support the woman who tosses in fitful sleep as a dozer
strips her mountains under cover of dark, who wakes
to thunder, boulders tumbled upon her baby in his bed.

Revile the judgment of life's worth in coal country,
a fine levied at fifteen thousand, less than the price
of a good pickup truck, how the law measures a baby's life.

Spare me the postmodern pout, the academic angst.
Travel ruined roads, moonscape mountains, failed farms
and ponder judicial disregard, mindful
of a poet's work, the naming of what matters.

James Still Leaves Wolfpen

> Trembling, I listened: the summer sun
> Had the chill of snow;
> For I knew she was telling the bees of one
> Gone on the journey we all must go!
> —John Greenleaf Whittier

Did anyone think
to tell the bees? Beltane dawned
and they were busy at fencerows
hung with blackberry lace
and honeysuckle twining sweet.

Did anyone think
to drape the hive? Hang an inky
crepe upon the skep? Beltane bloomed.
Were May baskets, the bright morning
custom, confused with memorials?

Did anyone think
to tell the bees? They surely were
the playfellows of his youth . . . who
danced Maypoles on Beltane morning,
clothed in garments of ballads.

Did anyone think
to lift the hive? Heave both boxes
the instant he was carried
from house to hollowed hillside
to reside eternal guardian of Troublesome?

Driving with the Dead

The little bus ate the road, rose toward the sky,
topped the mountain, perched on the edge before
falling toward the valley, white lines clicked
in rhythm to Mickey's drums, tape deck humming,
there is a road, no simple highway,
between the dawn and the dark of the night.
The mist gathered, fell in a steady drum
on the roof, merged to rivers on glass.
Truck tire spray, like white angel wings,
washed us, on our flight through the dark.

The author's great-great uncle, James S. Thomason, and friend, St. Louis. c. 1915

Dust

I am teary this morning, not with longing
but with the dust of dying summer, whirled up in the wake
of county machines trying to tame the yellow ditch rows,
trailed by tractors as farmers glean the last scant hay
as a wrinkled veil reddens the ridgetop, a perjury of promised rain.
My ridge life perched near woods, rusty dogwoods, and fox bark
is my grandfather's life far from paved road bustle.
My road is paved, but my well tastes of limestone
crisp and cold, like his well where we drew
long plungers to swirl in galvanized buckets.
In Dad's house on the raw edge of suburbia, town water
smelled of bleach and hot tar, not bedrock.
Past our house at the end of the street, town dropped off
to deep hollows and steep fields, a bridge to where night
dripped like fire when the rains still came.

Hunkering Down

the smell of dirt, always
the smell of dirt
—Kathryn Stripling Byer

In the half-light of winter when skies hang heavy
and souls seek sunlight, I walk out, let the cold clean
and lift me, discover what the snow drapes and reveals:
rectangular holes of woodpeckers lodged in long-dead trees,
green crowns of mistletoe in stately oaks, turkey-scratch
and doe-step to be scried for wisdom.

Hunkering down with books and quilts before hearth and fire,
rest the body, grow the soul. Come earth thaw, the smell of dirt
presses me down and down, heat diminishes me until I walk out
of a night, seek respite from the angry eye of summer.

My bones cannot forget clouded places
of misty days and wind-spirited nights
where elders nod, children huddle in furs,
and fireshine glitters harp strings in great halls
while winter howls and golden eyes lurk in the dark.

Bluegrass Festival

Slagle's Pasture, Tennessee

After midnight, spotlights dimmed,
the hardy play until dawn. A shiny case
from the trunk of a Volvo joins a case
tied with twine. They rosin up the same,
draw sweet notes on a long bow,
fast runs throw up white flakes
to tickle the fiddler's nose or dust
the beard of another. "Fox on the Run,"
hot and fast, working it. "Wheel Hoss"
on the mandolin of a tie-dye picker wandered
over from a nearby tent. A little moonshine,
some sipping whiskey, some sly weed
from a home harvested patch,
bring on the music, let it loose
to circle the campground, put paid performers
to shame, forget politics, run to the ridgetops,
and settle peace across the pasture.

The author's mother and friends. The inscription on the back reads,
"The Tennessee Fox Hunters, Pine Grove, Tennessee. 1945."

Notes

"Poor Valley Pilgrims": The Carter Family and others participated in recording sessions known as the "Big Bang of Country Music."

"Black Mountain Breakdown": Three-year-old Jeremy Davidson was killed when a boulder from an illegal strip mine plunged over 600 feet from the top of the Black Mountain and crashed through the side of his family's home in Inman, Virginia.

Acknowledgments

The author gratefully acknowledges the publishers of the following journals, in which some of these poems previously appeared, sometimes in earlier forms:

A! Magazine ("Bluegrass Festival," "Dismissal," "Jones and Thomason, General Merchandise," "Walking Boundaries," "What Matters"); *Appalachian Heritage* ("Black Mountain Breakdown," "Summer Rain"); *Appalachian Journal* ("James Still Leaves Wolfpen"); *Broad River Review* ("The Color of Loss," "Close Order," "Glitter"); *Nantahala Review* ("Tonic"); *Now & Then* ("The Grace of Risen Dough"); *Pine Mountain Sand and Gravel* ("Domestic Arts," "Expatriate," "Kindergarten"); *Shaking Like a Mountain* ("Poor Valley Pilgrims"); *Shenandoah* ("The Ryman Auditorium, 1965"); *Southern Ledger/South Poet* ("A Poet's Work"); *Still* ("Hunkering Down").

"A Poet's Work" and "Black Mountain Breakdown" appear in *We All Live Downstream: Writings on Mountaintop Removal,* ed. Jason Howard (Louisville, KY: Motes Books, 2009).

"A Transplant Leaves Minnesota, 1973" appear in *MOTIF Vol. 2: Come What May, an anthology of writing about chance*, ed. Marianne Worthington (Louisville, KY: Motes Books, 2011).

"A Poet's Work" and "Dust" appear in *The Southern Poetry Anthology, Volume III: Contemporary Appalachia*, ed. Jesse Graves, Paul Ruffin, and William Wright (Huntsville, TX: Texas Review Press, 2010).

"The Ryman Auditorium, 1965" appears in *The Southern Poetry Anthology, Volume VI: Tennessee*, ed. Jesse Graves, Paul Ruffin, and William Wright (Huntsville, TX: Texas Review Press, 2013).

"The Big Beautiful" appears in the novel *The Big Beautiful*, by Pamela Duncan (New York: Dial Press Trade Paperback, 2007).

Index of First Lines

Kentucky Voices

CPSIA information can be obtained at www.ICGtesting.com
Printed in the USA
BVOW07s0952140714

358844BV00001B/3/P